Samuel de Champlain

Liz Sonneborn

Franklin Watts
A Division of Scholastic Inc.
New York • Toronto • London • Auckland • Sydney
Mexico City • New Delhi • Hong Kong
Danbury, Connecticut

Note to readers: Definitions for words in **bold** can be found in the Glossary at the back of this book.

Photographs ©: Bridgeman Art Library International Ltd., London/New York: 44 (MOU 115125/ Philip Mould, Historical Portraits Ltd., London, UK/ Private Collection); Canadian Museum of Civilization: 32 (S94-37607), 47 (S94-13240); Corbis-Bettmann: 40 (Nathan Benn), 18 (Raymond Gehman), 5 top, 11, 24, 26, 34, 35, 41, 52; Liaison Agency, Inc.: 8, 9, (B. Rieger); Library of Congress: 42, 50; North Wind Picture Archives: 2, 17, 29, 31, 36, 49; Robert Holmes Photography: 20, 53; Stock Montage, Inc.: 5 bottom, 12, 22, 23, 28, 33, 38, 46; Wolfgang Käehler: 6.

Cover illustration by: Stephen Marchesi

The illustration on the cover shows Samuel de Champlain in New France. The photograph opposite the title page shows a statue of Champlain at the Chateau Frontenac in Quebec.

Visit Franklin Watts on the Internet at:
http://publishing.grolier.com

Library of Congress Cataloging-in-Publication Data

Sonneborn, Liz.
    Samuel de Champlain / Liz Sonneborn.
        p.   cm.— (Watts Library)
    Includes bibliographical references (p.) and index.
    ISBN 0-531-11978-5 (lib. bdg.)   0-531-16580-9 (pbk.)
    1. Champlain, Samuel de, 1567–1635—Juvenile literature. 2. Explorers—America—Biography—Juvenile literature. 3. Explorers—France—Biography—Juvenile literature. 4. New France—Discovery and exploration—French—Juvenile literature. 5. America—Discover and exploration—French—Juvenile literature. [1. Champlain, Samuel de, 1567–1635. 2. Explorers. 3. America—Discovery and exploration. 4. New France—Discovery and exploration.] I. Title. II. Series.
F1030.1 .S69 2001
971.01'13'092—dc21
                                    [B]
                            00-043782

Contents

Parc du Bic, located on the south shore of the St. Lawrence River, is one of the beautiful places in Canada that Champlain explored.

Chapter One

The Father of New France

"As for the country itself, it is beautiful and agreeable, and it brings all sorts of grain and seed to maturity. There are in it all the varieties of trees . . . and many fruits . . . which are quite good. There are also several sorts of useful herbs and roots. Fish are plentiful in the rivers, along which are meadows and game in vast quantity." In 1632, French explorer Samuel de Champlain wrote these words about the lands surrounding the settlement of Quebec in the area the French then called **Canada**. Nearly three decades before, he had adopted this beautiful wilderness as his new home.

Champlain was a man of many talents. He was an accomplished sailor. He was a great mapmaker. He was a skilled writer and artist. But Champlain is now best remembered for his efforts to build a French **colony** in Canada. This mission has earned him the name "the Father of **New France**" and "the Founder of Canada."

A Seaman by Birth

Champlain was born in about 1575 in Brouage, an oceanside town in southern France. At the time, Brouage was a busy seaport full of ships and sailors from throughout Europe. Many people came to the city to buy salt found in nearby marshlands. There were no refrigerators then, so one of the best ways people could preserve fresh meat and fish was to place them in salt.

In his many books, Champlain left few details about his youth. He did, however, once write, "From my childhood, the art of navigation has won my love." Growing up in Brouage gave him plenty of opportunity to meet sailors and watch them at work. He also

undoubtedly learned about ships and sailing from his father, Antoine, and his uncle, Guillaume Allene—both of whom were sea captains.

Sailing to Spain

Champlain's first career was not in sailing, but in the military. In his twenties, he joined the French king's army and helped fight off Spaniards who were invading France. In 1598, the French succeeded, and Champlain's army was disbanded.

People can visit the ruins of the ancient seaport of Brouage, France, where Champlain was born.

Unemployed, Champlain turned to his Uncle Guillaume for help. Guillaume had been hired to ship some of the Spanish troops home, and he invited his nephew to come with him. On the way to Spain, Champlain learned to sail a large ship and speak Spanish.

Champlain had good reason to go to Spain. He wanted to travel to the **West Indies,** a group of islands south of Florida that were then claimed by the king of Spain. Champlain hoped to join the annual Spanish expedition that carried **goods** to and from the islands. While there, he planned to learn as much as he could about the West Indies. When he came home, he would make a report to Henri IV, the king of France. The report, Champlain probably thought, might encourage the king to fund an expedition of his own.

In the late sixteenth century, France had all but given up on exploring North America. The country was involved in several wars, so the king did not have much money to spend on exploration. He also remembered the voyages of French explorer Jacques Cartier. In the 1530s and 1540s, Cartier made three trips up the St. Lawrence River, the largest waterway in present-day eastern Canada. Because of Cartier, France was able to claim the lands along the river.

Still, Cartier's voyages, particularly his final one in 1541, were considered disappointing. On his last trip, Cartier attempted to build a settlement. Cartier and his crew were surprised by the region's brutally cold weather. During their first winter, more than half of the crew died. The survivors,

Cartier's Canada

Jacques Cartier was the first to use the term *Canada*—an American Indian word meaning "village"—to describe the lands watered by the St. Lawrence River.

including Cartier, returned home. Adding to his embarrassment, the shiny yellow rocks Cartier brought back and said were gold were really pyrite—a worthless mineral often called "fool's gold." The journey was such a disaster that, for more than fifty years, France's rulers largely lost interest in Canada.

The West Indies

Champlain drew this picture of an animal in the West Indies. What animal do you think it is?

With his uncle's help, Champlain got a job on a Spanish ship. In January 1599, he set off on the first of twenty-one voyages across the Atlantic Ocean. After six weeks, he arrived in the West Indies. As he would on later voyages, Champlain played close attention to everything around him. He drew maps of

the islands he visited, and he drew pictures of the unfamiliar plants and animals he saw.

The outgoing Champlain also learned about his surroundings by talking to the people he met. On a side trip to Puerto Rico, for instance, he struck up a friendship with a Spanish-speaking man. The man told Champlain all about a recent attack the English had made on the Spanish town of San Juan. During his trip, Champlain also visited Mexico for a month. He later wrote that "a more beautiful country could not be seen or desired."

No doubt thrilled by his journey, Champlain returned to France to find his Uncle Guillaume on his deathbed. In his will, Guillaume left Champlain his houses and his land. The inheritance made Champlain a wealthy man. He was now free to devote himself to the life of travel and adventure he craved.

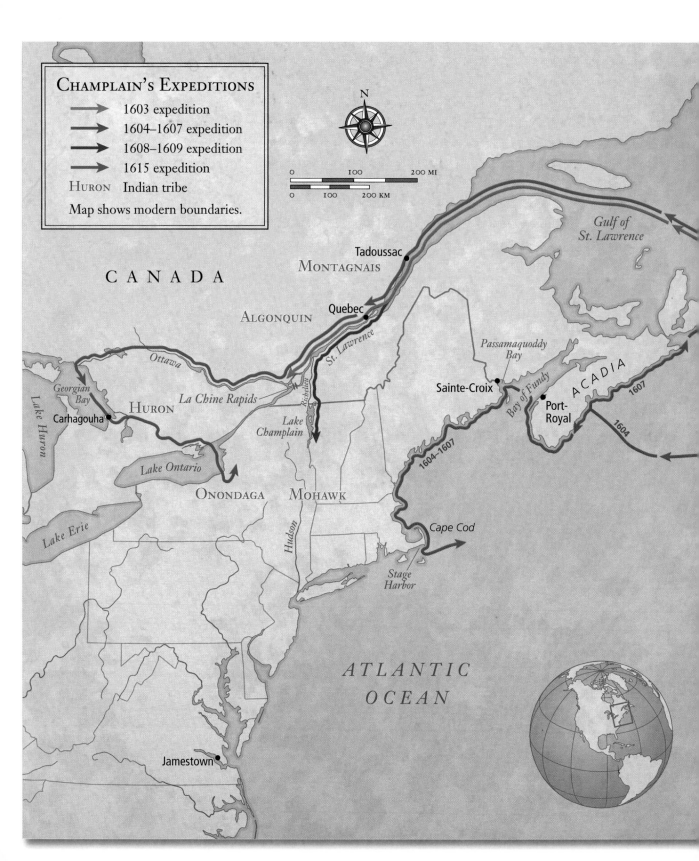

CHAMPLAIN'S EXPEDITIONS

→ 1603 expedition
→ 1604–1607 expedition
→ 1608–1609 expedition
→ 1615 expedition
HURON Indian tribe

Map shows modern boundaries.

N

0   100   200 MI
0   100   200 KM

Gulf of
St. Lawrence

CANADA

Tadoussac

MONTAGNAIS

Quebec

ALGONQUIN

Passamaquoddy
Bay

ACADIA

Ottawa

St. Lawrence

Sainte-Croix

Bay of Fundy

1607

Georgian
Bay

La Chine Rapids

Richelieu

Port-
Royal

1604

Lake
Huron

Carhagouha

HURON

Lake
Champlain

Lake Ontario

ONONDAGA

MOHAWK

1604–1607

Lake Erie

Hudson

Cape Cod

Stage
Harbor

ATLANTIC
OCEAN

Jamestown

Chapter Two

On to Canada

In 1603, Champlain received an exciting offer. A loud and burly sea captain named François Pont-Gravé asked him to join an expedition to the St. Lawrence River in Canada. Pont-Gravé probably invited Champlain because he was a mapmaker and a writer. He had demonstrated both skills in a short book on his voyage to the West Indies.

Pont-Gravé's expedition was funded by Aymar de Chaste. The French king had given De Chaste the exclusive right to trade with the American Indians living along the St. Lawrence. De Chaste's **monopoly** made French fishers furious.

Although the French king had little interest in Canada after Cartier's expeditions, fishers had continued to travel to the North American coast. They could make a decent living by catching and drying fish and then returning to France to sell their catch. While drying their fish on the shore, the fishers got to know the American Indians who lived nearby. They began to trade with one another. Through these early encounters, these American Indians came to see the French as their friends.

Soon the fishers developed a profitable business in beaver furs. The American Indians gave them furs in exchange for European goods, such as metal pots and knives. The fishers then sold the furs in Europe for a high price. At the time, fashionable Europeans enjoyed wearing wide-brimmed felt hats made from beaver pelts. The fishers soon discovered that there was more money to be made in furs than fish. With the king's support, De Chaste now hoped to take all the **fur trade** profits for himself.

Up the St. Lawrence

On May 26, 1603, Champlain, Pont-Gravé, and his crew arrived at Tadoussac, a trading post the French established on the St. Lawrence River. The next day, Champlain and Pont-Gravé went to meet with the Montagnais, the American Indians the French traded with most often then. Accompanying the explorers were two Montagnais men whom Pont-Gravé had taken to France the year before.

Champlain drew this map of the Tadoussac trading post. He labeled items with letters. In this map, "B" is a harbor and "N" is a pond.

Before Anadabijin, a powerful Montagnais leader, one of the Montagnais with Champlain told of his adventure in France. He talked of the French king's promise to help the Montagnais battle their worst American Indian enemies, the **Iroquois**. According to Champlain, Anadabijin announced that "they ought to be very glad to have His Majesty for their great friend. [The other Montagnais] answered with one voice, saying Ho, ho, ho, which is to say, yes, yes." Champlain and Pont-Gravé then joined the Montagnais for a huge

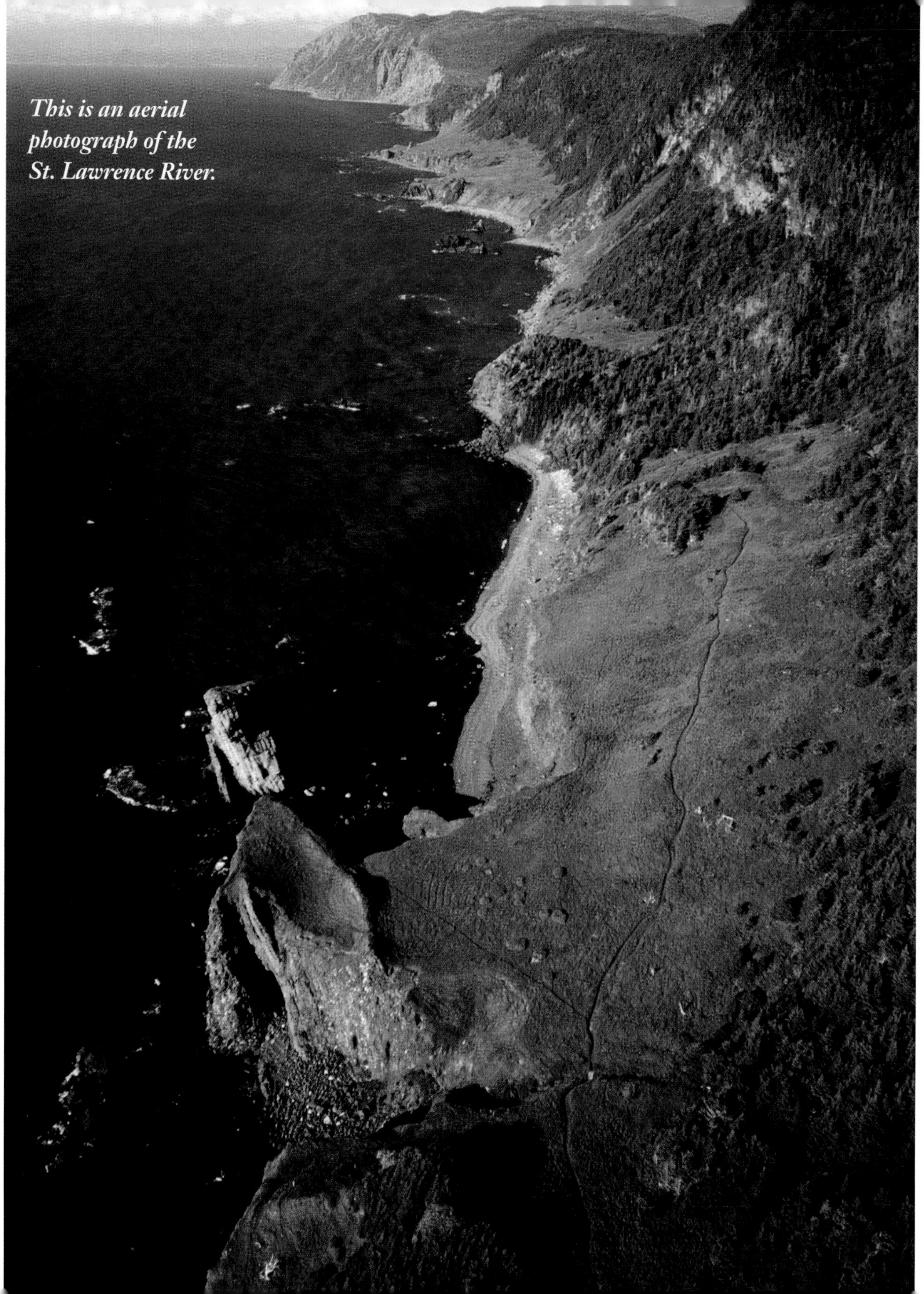

This is an aerial photograph of the St. Lawrence River.

feast of "eight or ten kettles" of moose, bear, seal, and beaver meat.

Assured of the Montagnais's friendship, Champlain set off to explore the St. Lawrence River. He traveled more than 400 miles (644 kilometers) to present-day Montreal, covering the same territory Cartier had decades before. But, keeping his eyes and ears open, Champlain learned plenty of new information about the region.

Champlain returned to Tadoussac and stayed with the Montagnais until the end of the summer of 1603. As the weather began to turn colder, the French crew loaded their ships with fish and furs and headed home. In France, Champlain wrote a second short book, *Des Sauvages*. It told about the rivers he had traveled, the lands he had seen, and the American Indians he had met. Although brief, Champlain's trip had been long enough to convince him that his fortunes lay in New France.

Sailing to Acadia

Champlain did not have to wait long for a chance to return. In 1604, he was asked to join the expedition of merchant Pierre du Gua, Sieur de Monts. De Chaste had died, and the king had given De Monts the fur trade monopoly. De Monts thought the weather in Tadoussac was too cold, so he sent his men farther south to an area they called **Acadia**. This region included parts of what are now the Canadian **provinces** of Nova Scotia and New Brunswick and the eastern part of Maine.

How Acadia Got Its Name

Acadia was probably named after Arcadia, a fabled paradise described by the ancient Greeks.

Part of what Champlain called Acadia is now a United States National Park. This photograph shows a section of the park along the coast of Maine.

De Monts, Champlain, his old friend Pont-Gravé, and a crew of between 80 and 120 people arrived in Acadia in May 1604. On orders of the king, they were to establish a permanent settlement. Champlain scouted out the right location. He and De Monts chose an island near Passamaquoddy Bay that they named Sainte-Croix—meaning "Holy Cross." "[W]ithout loss of time, the Sieur de Monts proceeded to set the workmen to build houses for our residence, and allowed me to draw up the plan for the settlement," Champlain wrote.

Despite the crew's hard work, they found little comfort when winter came. "The cold was . . . more extreme than in France, and lasted much longer," noted Champlain. Many of the party came down with **scurvy**, a disease caused by a lack of vitamin C. Thirty-five died while another twenty were seriously ill. To make matters worse, the ship of food and supplies due from France in the spring was late. They were almost ready to give up on Sainte-Croix when the supply ship finally arrived in June 1605.

Mapping New England

After the grueling winter, all agreed they needed to find a better spot for their settlement. Naming Champlain his first officer, De Monts took an expedition south all the way to Cape Cod, Massachusetts. As they traveled down the coast of New England, Champlain took careful note of the geography. His maps of the area were the most accurate made in the seventeenth century.

Although Champlain and De Monts found some excellent sites, De Monts insisted that they return north and build their new settlement at Port-Royal on Nova Scotia. Piece by piece, the men took down a few of the buildings at Sainte-Croix and put them back together at Port-Royal. Champlain made his own small garden and pond for trout. "We often went there to pass the time," he wrote of this special place. The winter was less harsh, but scurvy still took the lives of twelve more people.

Champlain at Plymouth

Fifteen years after Champlain first explored the coast of what is now Massachusetts, the Pilgrims built the English settlement of Plymouth.

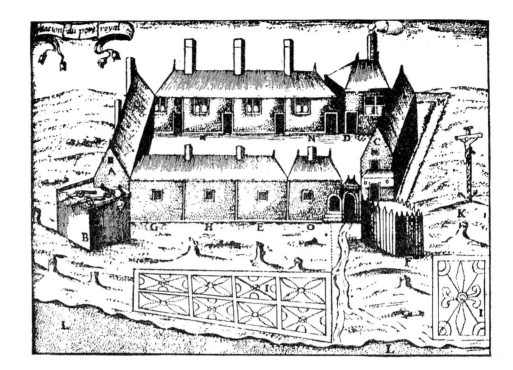

Champlain drew this picture of the settlement of Port-Royal. The section labeled "D" is Champlain and Pont-Gravé's home.

Battle at Stage Harbor

In the summer of 1606, Champlain and Pont-Gravé took another voyage along the New England coast. The American Indians they met were generally friendly. To show they had come in peace, the French offered them gifts of food and European goods. At Stage Harbor in Massachusetts, though, they met with disaster. Four or five members of Champlain's crew were camping on the beach when they were attacked and killed by four hundred local American Indians. The French took their brutal revenge by kidnapping a group of warriors and strangling and stabbing them to death.

The crew returned to Port-Royal for what would be their last winter there. In May 1607, a French ship arrived with bad

The Order of Good Cheer

To keep spirits up during the long winter months of 1606, Champlain created "The Order of Good Cheer." Each day, during a little ceremony, a chain was placed around the neck of one of the people at Port-Royal. That person was then responsible for hunting and fishing for the day's food. Everyone competed to bring in the best meal. Champlain wrote that, because of the game, "we spent the winter very pleasantly, and had good [food]."

news. Rival fur merchants, angered at De Monts's monopoly, pressured the king to end it. Faced with competition from these other traders, De Monts could not make enough money to fund his settlement. In the autumn of 1607, De Monts's colony was disbanded. Champlain had no choice but to return to France.

Samuel de Champlain

King Henry IV of France

Chapter Three

Building Quebec

Back in France, Champlain devoted himself to one of the most important missions of his life—convincing De Monts and King Henri IV not to give up on New France. De Monts had spent a good deal of money trying to build a colony, and he had little to show for it. King Henri IV was also disappointed. De Monts's crew had not found gold or any other riches in New France that could add to the king's wealth.

The Meaning of Quebec

The word *Quebec* means "the narrows of the river" in the language of the Algonquin Indians.

Champlain argued that they had tried to build their settlement in the wrong place. He said they should abandon Acadia for the St. Lawrence River valley. On his 1603 expedition, Champlain had found what he thought was an ideal spot. Along a bend on the St. Lawrence was an area with rich soil and good fishing that could easily be defended from attackers. The Algonquin Indians called it "Quebec."

In this painting, Champlain is selecting the site of Quebec.

A New Settlement

Champlain's glowing description of Quebec won over De Monts and the king. De Monts agreed to fund another expedition, and the king renewed De Monts's trade monopoly for another year. De Monts was so confident in Champlain that he placed him in charge of the expedition, with Pont-Gravé as his second-in-command.

Champlain and Pont-Gravé arrived at Tadoussac on the St. Lawrence River in May 1608. From the start, everything seemed to go wrong. Spanish traders, angry at De Monts, took Pont-Gravé captive. Champlain had to promise to let them trade with nearby American Indians in exchange for his friend's release.

Soon Champlain and his crew headed up the river and set about building the Quebec settlement. A few members of the crew, convinced they would make more money working for rival traders, planned a **mutiny** to rebel against Champlain's leadership. One crew member confessed to Champlain that there was a plot brewing to kill him. Champlain arrested, tried, and hanged the ringleader and sent the others back to France to stand trial.

As winter set in, Champlain's luck grew even worse. The weather turned unusually cold, food supplies ran low, and scurvy began to spread. The French were barely surviving, but the Montagnais Indians were suffering even more. The hunting season ended early, leaving them with no food. A group of Montagnais men, women, and children showed up at Quebec,

Champlain drew this picture of his house in Quebec. He designed and built this home in 1608.

and they begged for help. "They looked like skeletons," wrote Champlain. He gave them some bread and beans from the crew's meager provisions.

The League of the Iroquois

In Champlain's time, the Iroquois were a confederacy of five tribes—the Mohawk, Seneca, Oneida, Onondaga, and Cayuga.

The Battle of Lake Champlain

When the weather improved, Champlain set about strengthening his friendship with the Montagnais. Six years before, he had agreed to help them fight the Iroquois, their worst enemies. Now the Montagnais and their American Indian **allies,** the Huron and the Algonquin, wanted Champlain to make good on his promise.

Champlain invited the allies' leaders to Quebec to plan a campaign against the Iroquois. Following American Indian custom, they performed ceremonies for five days in order to prepare themselves for war. Champlain, two other Frenchmen, and a war party of Montagnais, Huron, and Algonquin then set off for Iroquois territory. They traveled up the St. Lawrence River to the Richelieu River. It led them to a great lake, which Champlain named after himself.

Near Lake Champlain, Champlain's party met up with some two hundred Mohawk Indians on July 30, 1609. At the urging of his American Indian allies, Champlain stepped forward, loaded his musket with four balls, and shot at the Mohawk's three chiefs. Two fell dead, and the third died later

This illustration shows Champlain taking aim against the Mohawk Indians on July 30, 1609.

from his wounds. The warriors shot a few arrows back and forth, but the battle was essentially over. Although the Mohawk were fearsome fighters, they retreated. They had no guns, and they were terrified of them. This encounter marked the beginning of a long, angry relationship between the Iroquois and the French. For the next hundred years, the Iroquois would consider the French their enemies.

The 1610 Campaign

Champlain soon left for France, where he proudly told King Henri IV of his war victories. He then headed back to Quebec. In May 1610, he met with a party of sixty Montagnais eager for another battle with the Iroquois. Champlain and the Montagnais planned to join Huron and Algonquin warriors along the Richelieu River. But when they reached the river, they discovered the Huron and Algonquin had begun the attack on the Iroquois without them. On June 19, 1610, Champlain's party joined the fight. They stormed the Iroquois's fort, killing nearly all of their enemies. But

Champlain's American Indian allies also suffered many casualties. Champlain himself was wounded when an arrow struck his neck.

Returning to Quebec, Champlain was given the news that King Henri IV had been assassinated. He rushed back to France, where he spent the winter. While there, Champlain married the twelve-year-old Hélène Boullé on December 30, 1610. As was common at the time, her parents arranged the marriage. After several months, Champlain returned to Canada, leaving his bride behind in Paris.

After surviving a near shipwreck, Champlain arrived back in Quebec in May 1611. He headed farther inland up the St. Lawrence River to the La Chine Rapids. There, he wanted to build a new trading post that would be closer to Huron and Algonquin territory. De Monts's trade monopoly had run out, so now Champlain had to compete with other French traders.

Champlain was the first European to successfully ride the La Chine Rapids.

He promised the Huron and Algonquin to establish more trading posts in their lands, and he hoped that they would choose to deal only with him.

Champlain knew his allies valued courage above all else. Possibly to further win them over, he rode a canoe down the rapids—a trip that had already killed two members of

Champlain's Astrolabe

In 1867, a fourteen-year-old boy in Ontario, Canada, spotted a strange object on the ground. He had found what is said to be Champlain's **astrolabe** (shown above), a navigational instrument. While sailing, Champlain used the instrument to measure the angle between the sun and the horizon. From this measurement, he could determine his location. Champlain lost his astrolabe during his 1613 expedition, and the instrument was lost in the dirt for the next 254 years. Now Champlain's astrolabe is in the Canadian Museum of Civilization.

his crew. Unable to swim, Champlain must have found it difficult to hide his terror. "I assure you that even the bravest people in the world . . . could not [ride the rapids] without great apprehension," he later wrote.

Promoting Canada

In August 1611, Champlain headed back home. He was eager to see De Monts and sell him on his plan to build posts in Huron and Algonquin territory. De Monts was unable to get his monopoly renewed, and he told Champlain he could no longer fund Quebec. Just as it looked like Quebec might be abandoned forever, a new twelve-year royal monopoly was granted to Prince Henri de Condé in late 1612.

Champlain was not able to return to New France until 1613. He again met with American Indians at the La Chine Rapids, but his reception was chilly. They were angry that he had not come to the region the year before as he had promised. Champlain would have to work hard to regain their trust.

Returning to France in the winter, Champlain put the finishing touches on *Les Voyages* (1613), an account of his adventures in Canada from 1604 to 1612. The centerpiece of the book was a great map of New France. This map showed everything he had learned about its geography. He also decorated the book with pictures he drew of American Indians, plants, fish, and great whales. He hoped that these images of the exotic people and wildlife he had encountered would attract new investors to keep his dreams for Quebec alive.

LES VOYAGES
DV SIEVR DE CHAMPLAIN
XAINTONGEOIS, CAPITAINE
ordinaire pour le Roy,
en la marine.

DIVISEZ EN DEVX LIVRES.
ou,

IOVRNAL TRES-FIDELE DES OBSERVA-tions faites és defcouuertures de la Nouuelle France: tant en la defcriptiõ des terres, coftes, riuieres, ports, haures, leurs hauteûrs, & plufieurs declinaffons de la guide-aymant; qu'en la creãce des peuples, leur fuperftition, façon de viure & de guerroyer: enrichi de quantité de figures.

Enfemble deux cartes geografiques: la premiere feruant à la nauigation, dreffée felon les compas qui nordeftent, fur lefquels les mariniers nauigent: l'autre en fon vray Meridien, auec fes longitudes & latitudes: à laquelle eft adioufté le voyage du deftroict qu'ont trouué les Anglois, au deffus de Labrador, depuis le 53e. degré de latitude, iufques au 63e. en l'an 1612. cerchans vn chemin par le Nord, pour aller à la Chine.

A PARIS,
Chez IEAN BERJON, rue S. Iean de Beauuais, au Cheual volant, & en fa boutique au Palais, à la gallerie des prifonniers.

M. DC. XIII.
AVEC PRIVILEGE DV ROY.

The title page of Champlain's Les Voyages *(1613)*

This illustration shows colonists landing at Jamestown, Virginia. In Champlain's time, Jamestown was a more successful colony than Quebec.

Chapter Four

A Visit to Huronia

By 1613, Champlain knew the pressure was on: If he was to build a sizable permanent colony in New France, it was now or never. He was faced with rival French traders and new European competitors. The English had already established a settlement—Jamestown in Virginia. Dutch traders were also making headway along the Hudson River in what is now New York.

For two years, Champlain stayed in France, working hard to gather enough funds to keep his colony going. During this time, he also recruited four priests to go to Canada with him. These **missionaries** were charged with teaching France's American Indian allies about Christianity. Like most Europeans of time, Champlain and the priests believed it was their moral duty to convert American Indians to their own religion.

Fighting the Onondaga

The Huron traded beaver pelts for European goods such as hatchets, knives, and fishhooks.

By May 1615, Champlain was back in New France. His first order of business was to go to **Huronia**—the land of the Huron Indians. Two years before, he had promised to visit the Huron. Champlain did not want to disappoint them. He

needed to keep the Huron happy because they had become important partners in the fur trade.

The Huron were not hunters, but farmers. They traded corn and other crops to hunting tribes in the north, where the beaver with the thickest furs were found. Working as middlemen, the Huron could supply the French with huge numbers of the best beaver pelts available.

Champlain traveled inland for three months before he reached a great lake—now called Lake Huron after his allies. He then toured several Huron villages. He concluded, "It is a pleasure to travel in this country, so fair and fertile it is." Visiting the Huron, Champlain quickly learned that they wanted him to join them in another battle against the Iroquois. In the village of Carhagoua, he started gathering up a force of warriors, but he grew frustrated with their insistence on feasting and dancing first. Champlain was more understanding of American Indian ways than many Europeans of his day. Yet, he had little patience for the elaborate ceremonies the Huron always performed before going to war.

The Huron, in turn, grew annoyed with Champlain's military instructions. In European war campaigns, a commander sought the advantage of sneak attack. As the two hundred Huron warriors moved into Iroquois territory, Champlain insisted they all be quiet, so they could surprise the Iroquois. The Huron completely ignored him. When they came upon the fort of the Onondaga—one of the Iroquois tribes—the Huron freely called out insults, not caring that it gave their

The Wendat

The Huron called themselves the Wendat. Like the Iroquois, they were a confederacy of several tribes.

Champlain's illustration of the French–Huron attack on the Onondaga shows how well-protected their fort was.

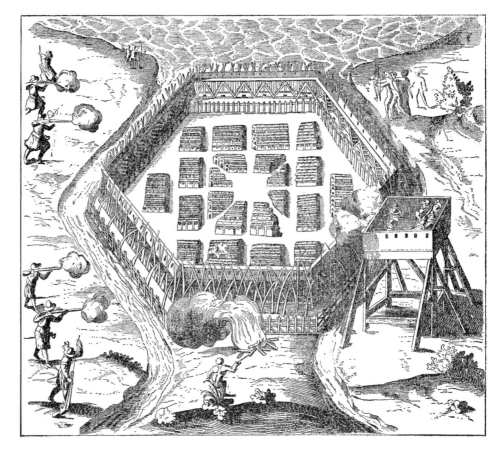

position away. This made Champlain furious. He did not understand that, to the Huron, these taunts had great meaning. In their rules of warfare, humiliating their enemies was as important as physically hurting them.

On October 10, 1615, the French–Huron assault on the Onondaga began. Champlain quickly grew irritated with the Huron, who refused to battle in an orderly way. They preferred a free-for-all style of fighting very foreign to Champlain. Even worse, the Onondaga had learned something from the Iroquois's past experiences with French guns.

Their fort, with its thirty-foot walls, was hard to penetrate. From their protected position, they killed and wounded many of Champlain's force. Champlain himself took arrows in his knee and leg.

In the end, the Huron were forced to retreat. Champlain and the Huron viewed this battle differently. When Europeans fought other Europeans, they generally did so to take control of their enemy's territory. Champlain considered the battle an utter failure because the Huron were unable to take over the Onondaga's fort. His Huron allies generally did not fight for territory—they fought to remind their enemies how powerful they were. The Huron had killed a number of Onondaga, so in their eyes, the campaign was a success.

Winter Among the Huron

Temporarily crippled by his wounds, Champlain had to be carried back to Huronia. He asked the Huron to take him back to Quebec for the winter, but they refused. Most likely, they were afraid the Iroquois might try to take revenge on Champlain and kill him on his way home. If Champlain were murdered, the Huron feared they could lose the French as their **ally**.

Although he grumbled about it, Champlain had no choice but to spend the winter of 1615–1616 in the Huron villages. He took the opportunity to study the Huron and learn more about how they lived. He observed, for instance, that their villages were a collection of large oval shaped dwellings known

Iroquois longhouses were constructed from young trees that were bent in a half-moon shape and then covered with bark.

Huron Jewelry

Champlain wrote that Huron women wore strings of shell beads that weighed as much as 12 pounds (5 kilograms).

as **longhouses**. He wrote that in each longhouse "there will be twelve fires which make twenty-four households." The houses were comfortable, but he noted that with only small smoke holes in the roof, "there is smoke in good earnest, causing many to have great eye troubles."

During his stay in the Huron villages, Champlain learned to like many Huron foods. He often ate cornmeal bread, red beans, and boiled corn flavored with blueberries or raspberries. However, he wrote that the "Migan . . . is the best to my taste." This favorite dish was a soup made of corn and roasted meat or fish.

Champlain also was impressed by the cleverness of their hunters. He described how the Huron used fences forming a

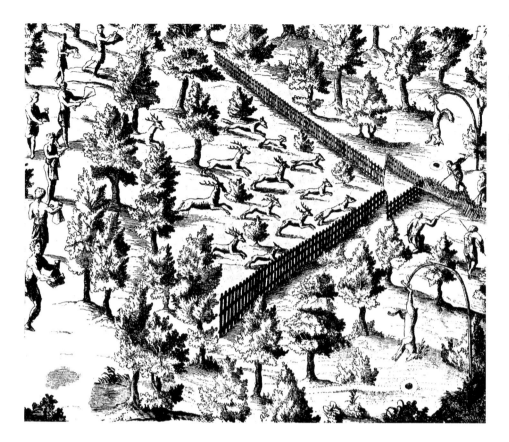

In October 1615, Champlain observed a Huron deer hunt near what is now Kingston, Ontario. Then he drew this picture of the hunt.

large funnel to catch deer. A few hunters, making as much noise as possible, would drive a group of deer into the funnel's point. There, other hunters would be waiting with spears in hand to kill the frightened animals.

In the spring of 1616, Champlain was able to set off for Quebec, accompanied by one of the Huron's leaders, D'Arontal. Despite the defeat by the Onondaga, the expedition had been valuable. Champlain was able to explore much of Huronia and the surrounding area. By living with the Huron, he also helped to cement his friendship with these important trading partners.

The Feast of the Dead

While wintering among the Huron, Champlain witnessed their burial customs, and he drew this picture of them. He wrote that when a Huron died, "They take the body of the deceased, wrap it in furs, cover it very neatly with tree-bark, then lift it up on four posts." Once every ten years, the Huron opened the bark coffins of the recently dead during their most sacred ceremony, the Feast of the Dead. Huron women first unearthed their relatives' bones, "which they cleanse[d] and [made] quite clean." The corpses were then reburied in a great pit filled with "necklaces, wampum [shell bead] chains, tomahawks, kettles, sword-blades," and other valuables. The bones were then placed atop these valuables and covered with earth. The ceremony ended with a great feast. The Huron believed that this ritual freed their relatives' souls to travel to the land of the dead.

Champlain's trip to Huronia was his last journey into unknown territory. He was now well into his forties, and he was too weary to travel the difficult journeys he had loved as a young man. As he headed back to France in the autumn of 1616, Champlain left his days as an explorer behind him. For many years to come, however, he would remain New France's most vocal and passionate champion.

King Louis XIII of France

Chapter Five

Final Days

In 1618, Champlain gave King Louis XIII, the successor of Henri IV, a report that set forth his ideas for the future of Canada. After reminding the king of his long years of hard work, Champlain told King Louis XIII of all the wonderful things the region had to offer. There were fish from the lakes and rivers, timber from forests, and crops of all kinds from the rich farmland. To take advantage of these resources, Champlain said the French needed to persuade people to stay there permanently. He proposed that the king help send three hundred

In Champlain's last years, he spent much of his time persuading people to support Quebec.

families, three hundred soldiers to protect them, and fifteen more priests to convert the American Indians.

Champlain's ambitious plan impressed many powerful people in France. Yet, they did little to help him realize it. For nearly a decade after Champlain's return to Quebec in 1620, the monopoly on trade in Canada continually changed hands. With each shift, Champlain had to reassert his authority just to keep others from taking control of Quebec. It became clear, too, that these financial backers were not interested in spending the money to build the colony Champlain envisioned. They were happy operating a few trading posts, getting no more than a few shiploads of furs each year in return.

Without more funds, Champlain had little hope of attracting colonists. As a result, only sixty-four people lived in all of New France in 1627. In comparison, England's Virginia settlement now boasted a population of more than two thousand.

The English Threat

Early 1628 found Champlain in Quebec, and he faced several of the worst emergencies of his career. Relations with his American Indian allies were going badly. Two Frenchmen had

been killed the previous fall, probably by the Montagnais. Champlain insisted the Montagnais turn over the murderers, but the Montagnais were hesitant. In their culture, a murderer was usually punished by giving some of his or her possessions to the victim's family. The French were likely to execute a killer—a punishment the Montagnais considered extreme. As the Montagnais and the French argued about what to do, tensions grew. Both sides became uneasy with one another.

Even worse for Champlain, the food stores of the French were running dangerously low. With the annual supply ship from France overdue, the French at Quebec patched together a small boat to take a party downriver to ask for emergency supplies from the traders at Tadoussac. While Champlain was nervously waiting, a messenger arrived in Quebec. He said he

This model shows Champlain's second house in Quebec. This home was built in 1628.

47

had seen six strange sailing ships up the St. Lawrence River. The French hoped these were supply ships from home, but they soon learned the truth. They were English ships, commanded by David Kirke. Unknown to the colonists at Quebec, France and England had gone to war. Kirke and his brothers, Louis and Thomas, had now brought the conflict to North America by attacking and capturing Tadoussac.

David Kirke sent a message to Champlain. Though polite in tone, Kirke's letter was not friendly. He told Champlain he had blockaded the St. Lawrence so no French supply ships could get through. Knowing they needed food, Kirke wrote, "I shall more easily obtain what I desire—which is to take your settlement." Champlain wrote his own courteous reply. He acknowledged the French were low on supplies but told Kirke Quebec's "defenders [are not] destitute of courage." Champlain's promise to fight and fight hard put Kirke off. For the time being, he decided not to attack Quebec.

Quebec Surrenders

Champlain's problems were far from over. The French at Quebec now had to face a long, cold winter without any more supplies. They had to make do with corn, peas, nuts, berries, roots, fish, and wild animal meat. By the spring of 1629, they were starving. Champlain considered attacking the Iroquois so the French could steal some of their corn. The French, though, had so little gunpowder that if they carried out the raid, they would have none left for hunting.

The Iroquois corn harvest must have tempted the starving French.

In July 1629, Champlain received word that English ships were heading for Quebec. The last miserable year had shown Champlain that he now had no choice. He hoisted a white flag over Quebec and met with a messenger sent by Louis and Thomas Kirke. The messenger handed Champlain a letter insisting on total surrender of Quebec to the English. Champlain asked that his people be allowed to keep their belongings and safely return to France. When the English agreed, Champlain sadly surrendered his beloved Quebec.

The Last Voyage

In September 1629, Champlain boarded the Kirke brothers' ship and sailed to Tadoussac. From there, he was sent to England, where he learned that the war between France and

England had officially ended more than six months ago. Champlain was furious. The English had seized Quebec illegally, months after the peace treaty was signed.

In London, Champlain took up the matter with the French ambassador to England. He insisted that Quebec be returned to France. The ambassador took his complaint to the English king, but nothing happened. A frustrated and disappointed Champlain returned to France. He was determined to work from there for the return of Quebec.

While Champlain argued for his cause, he compiled his longest and most ambitious book, *Les Voyages* (1632). The book covered his experiences involving New France from 1604 to 1629. It also included *Treatise on Seamanship*, a brief supplement on navigation and conducting battles at sea. *Les Voyages* of 1632 also featured Champlain's last great map,

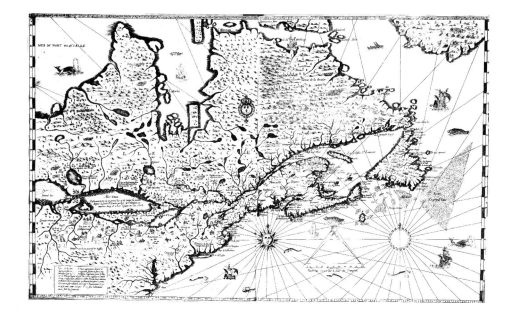

Champlain's map of 1632 shows the French settlements in North America founded between 1603 and 1629.

which summarized all the information he had learned on his journeys in New France.

A treaty signed on March 29, 1632, settled the question of what to do about Quebec. The English king agreed to return the settlement if the French king paid a debt he owed. The next year, Champlain set out for New France for the last time. His homecoming was hardly happy. While under English rule, the buildings at Quebec had all but fallen apart. The American Indian alliances he had built up so carefully had also been destroyed.

Champlain's final mission was difficult, but familiar. Again, he rallied the French to construct new buildings. Again, he slowly courted the goodwill of his American Indian allies. And again, he begged France to give him more support. After spending his last years trying to preserve his life's work, Champlain died at Quebec on Christmas Day in 1635.

Champlain's Legacy

After Champlain's death, Quebec survived, but it hardly thrived. Quebec remained only a small settlement and continued to get little funding from France. In 1663, New France finally received a much-needed boost when King Louis XIV made it a royal province. Soon afterward, he sent three thousand people to help build up New France into a more powerful colony.

Even with this help, the French settlements in North America grew much more slowly than those of the English. By

This drawing of Quebec shows how the settlement looked around the time of Champlain's death.

the mid-eighteenth century, the English were in a position to try to take over New France. A series of wars between the England and France ended with the French and Indian War (1754–1763). In this conflict, most of the American Indians involved fought on the side of the French. In keeping with the policies promoted by Champlain, the French had continued to work hard maintaining close alliances with their American

The Iroquois-Huron War

Allying themselves to Champlain had dire consequences for the Huron. With his help, they could battle their enemies, the powerful Iroquois. These battles and the Huron's success in the fur trade, however, made the Iroquois deter- mined to destroy them. In 1648, the Iroquois launched a devastat- ing military campaign, using Dutch guns against the Huron. Many Huron were killed, and the survivors were forced from their homeland.

Indian allies. Despite their help, the French lost the war to the English. In the peace treaty, France surrendered almost all its lands in North America to the English. Champlain's dream of a New France across the ocean had come to an end.

The influence of Champlain and other early French explorers, however, is still felt. Champlain's small settlement of Quebec is now a great city and the capital of the Canadian province of Quebec. Although most Canadians speak English, the majority of people in Quebec speak French. Fiercely proud of their French heritage, they continue to honor Champlain as a founder.

The National Assembly of Quebec is where the Canadian legislature meets.

Quebec's Population

Home to about 700,000 people, Quebec is the seventh largest city in modern Canada.

Timeline

1575	Born in Brouage, France
1595	Joins the French army
1599–1601	Travels to Spain, Cuba, Mexico, and the West Indies
1601	Inherits a large estate from his uncle
1603	Travels to Canada for the first time; explores the St. Lawrence River and Acadia; publishes *Des Sauvages*
1604–1607	Travels to Acadia; founds Sainte-Croix and Port-Royal; explores the New England coast
July 3, 1608	Founds the French settlement of Quebec
July 30, 1609	Joins the Montagnais, Huron, and Algonquin Indians in fighting the Iroquois at Lake Champlain
June 19, 1610	Fights his second battle against the Iroquois
December 27, 1610	Marries Hélène Boullé
October 10, 1615	Loses a battle against the Iroquois at present-day Syracuse, New York
Winter 1615–1616	Stays in the villages of the Huron
1618	Presents King Louis XIII with an ambitious plan for New France
July 1628	Resists an English takeover of Quebec
July 19, 1629	Surrenders Quebec to the English
March 29, 1632	France regains control of Quebec
1633	Returns to Quebec for the last time
December 25, 1635	Dies in Quebec

Glossary

Acadia—an area once claimed by France made up of portions of present-day Nova Scotia, New Brunswick, and the eastern part of Maine

alliance—an association formed by two or more groups for assistance and protection

ally (plural **allies**)—a person or group associated or united with another in a common purpose

Canada—in Champlain's day, the lands along the St. Lawrence River that were claimed by France; today, Canada is the large country north of the United States.

colony—a territory that is far away from the country that governs it

fur trade—the exchange of European goods for animal furs in colonial North America

goods—items that can be bought or sold

Huronia—the traditional territory of the Huron Indians

Iroquois—a confederacy of American Indian tribes who traditionally lived in what is now New York State. In Champlain's time, the Iroquois were a confederacy of five tribes—the Mohawk, Seneca, Oneida, Onondaga, and Cayuga.

longhouse—a large multi-family dwelling traditionally built by the Huron, Iroquois, and other related American Indian peoples in northern North America

missionary—a person who travels to another land to convert others to his or her religion

monopoly—the exclusive right to trade or sell goods in a specific area

mutiny—the overthrow of a leader by his or her followers

New France—the lands in North America claimed by France in the sixteenth, seventeenth, and eighteenth centuries

province—a part of a country having a government of its own

scurvy—a disease caused by a lack of vitamin C, common among sailors on long voyages

West Indies—a group of islands south of Florida that were claimed by the king of Spain during Champlain's time

To Find Out More

Books

Bial, Raymond. *The Huron*. Tarrytown, NY: Benchmark Books, 2000.

Coulter, Tony. *Jacques Cartier, Samuel de Champlain, and the Explorers of Canada*. New York: Chelsea House Publishers, 1993.

Hamilton, Janice. *Quebec*. Minneapolis, MN: Lerner Publications, 1996.

Rodgers, Barbara Radcliffe and Stillman D. Rodgers. *Canada*. Danbury, CT: Children's Press, 2000.

Sherrow, Victoria. *The Iroquois Indians*. New York: Chelsea House Publishers, 1993.

Organizations and Online Sites

"Canada Hall"

http://www.civilization.ca/cmc/cmceng/canp1eng.html

This virtual version of the Canadian Museum of Civilization's permanent exhibit offers information on early Canadian history, including everyday life in New France.

Canadian Museum of Civilization

100 Laurier Street

P.O. Box 3100

Station B

Hull, Quebec J8X 4H2

"Living in Canada in the Time of Champlain"

http://www.vmnf.civilization.ca/expos/champlain/indexeng.html

This Virtual Museum of New France exhibit describes how people lived in early Quebec and features photographs of all kinds of objects used at the settlement.

A Note on Sources

In writing this book, I owe a debt to the two most recent biographies of Champlain written in English: Samuel Morison's *Samuel de Champlain: Father of New France* (Little Brown, 1972) and Joe C. Armstrong's *Champlain* (Macmillan of Canada, 1987). Both authors have an affection for Champlain that any reader will find contagious. For the spelling and styling for the names of people and places, I've relied on Morison for guidance.

To get a sense of how Champlain's American Indian allies and enemies might have regarded him, I've turned to the work of the Canadian anthropologist Bruce G. Trigger, particularly his *Natives and Newcomers: Canada's "Heroic Age" Reconsidered* (McGill-Queen's University Press, 1985). For general background on New France, I've found W. J. Eccles's *France in America* (Michigan State University Press, rev. ed., 1990) especially helpful.

Of course, the best source on Champlain is Champlain himself. The most complete collection of Champlain's writings is editor H. P. Biggar's six-volume *Works of Samuel de Champlain* (University of Toronto Press, rev. ed., 1971).

I also want to thank Jean-Pierre Hardy, a historian at the Canadian Museum of Civilization, for his useful advice.

Liz Sonneborn

Index

Numbers in *italics* indicate illustrations.

About the Author

Liz Sonneborn is a writer and an editor, and she lives in Brooklyn, New York. A graduate of Swarthmore College, she specializes in books about the history and culture of American Indians and the biographies of noteworthy people in American history. She has written eighteen books for children and adults, including *A to Z of Native American Women* and *The New York Public Library's Amazing Native American History*. In researching *Samuel de Champlain*, she particularly enjoyed learning about the founding of Quebec, one of her favorite cities.

Samuel de Champlain